Memory Foundations for Reading
Visual Mnemonics for Sound/Symbol Relationships

◆ ◆ ◆

Regina G. Richards

Richards Educational Therapy Center, Inc.
Riverside, CA
ISBN 0-9661353-0-X

RET Center Press
190 E. Big Springs Road
Riverside, CA 92507

ISBN: 0-9661353-0-X

Richards, Regina G.

Memory Foundations for Reading. Visual Mnemonics for Sound/Sym-
bol Relationships/Regina G. Richards.

Includes bibliographical references.

ISBN 0-9661353-0-X

1. Learning, Psychology of. 2. Mnemonics. 3. Visual learning. 4. Phonics.

Gordon Sherman, M.D., director of the Dyslexia Research Laboratory at Beth Israel Deconess Medical Center in Boston, and 1996-98 President of the International Dyslexia Association was asked:

"Is there any magic bullet for dealing with the problem of dyslexia?"

His reply:

"No, but this is an incredibly exciting time. We know how to diagnose dyslexia accurately. We know how to treat it with these multisensory language techniques. We must let parents know they're available, though not easy. Teachers have to invest time to learn them and work with kids. But if there's any magic in the field, this is it."

—Interview of Dr. Gordon with People Magazine 9/22/97

Contents

Credits

Author:

Regina G. Richards, M.A.
          Educational Therapist

Contributing Authors/
Participants in Creating Mnemonics:

Staff at Richards Educational Therapy Center, Inc.:
Simone Acosta, Support Teacher
Deborah Eiseman, Educational Therapist
Susan Frazier, Music and Educational Therapist
Judy Love, Educational Therapist
Dindy Wheelock, M.S., Speech and Language Therapist

Art Work:

Christine Noah, Art Therapist (all pictures except those listed below)
Carol Brandon, (1.4, 2.1, 2.3, 3.3, 3.8)
Deborah Eiseman (1.2)
Kathy Foster (3.12)

Acknowledgements

We gratefully acknowledge *Remedial Training for Children with Specific Disability in Reading, Spelling, and Penmanship* by Anna Gillingham and Bessie Stillman (published by Educator's Publishing Service, Inc., 1960) for their fine sequence of introduction of phonograms and many of their fine ideas on multisensory teaching, especially the use of associations and key words.

We gratefully acknowledge the concept of the phonic mnemonic method of teaching reading as developed by Leland D. Michael, O.D., James W. King, O.D., and Arlene Moorhead and as utilized in the *MKM Reading Systems* (published by MKM Inc., South Dakota, 1978). The use of the MKM Reading Systems' materials has been a major influence in the development of our mnemonic program.

Foreword

I am pleased to be writing the foreword to the text on *Memory Foundations for Reading* by Regina G. Richards and the staff at the Richards Educational Therapy Center.

It has been my pleasure to work with this outstanding staff and to help in the rehabilitation of many exceptional students during the past several years. As a clinical neuropsychologist, it is often one of my tasks to define as exactly as possible the breakdown in reading skills of certain patients. Often there are functional and organic disabilities which interfere with the initial speech sound or phonemic analysis in these individuals. Until the child can utilize basic phonetic sounds in analyzing words, the reading process can never really begin.

In the text, a program is presented to circumvent the often deficient phonetic memory by taking advantage of specific visual mnemonic or memory techniques. In most children with dysfunctional phonetic skills, the visual memory processes are intact and may even be superior. Once phonetic skills have been encoded by these alternative methods, a major hurdle toward fluid reading has been surmounted. These simple and well thought out materials can provide the first step toward a program of reading reeducation as well as a basic for improvement in the child's often damaged self-image.

Wallace T. Cleaves, Ph.D.
Professor of Psychology
Licensed Psychologist in Clinical Neuropsychology

MFR
Preface

Most children, in the learning-to-read process, learn effortlessly and efficiently the association between sound and symbol. These associations form the foundations for their decoding and encoding skills which will make them fluent readers and spellers. A small group of children—most often those in slower reading groups—are unable, for any of a vast number of reasons, to make the basic linkages. For these children, both the young ones as well as others in remedial situations, MFR-*Memory Foundations for Reading*—was developed.

MFR teaches the initial steps of reading through a mnemonic system. The concept of mnemonics is not new. It is defined by Webster's Dictionary (Second College Edition, 1974) as "a technique or system of improving memory by the use of a certain formula." Many people are familiar with *"every good boy does fine"* for learning the notes of the musical scale. Some of us learn to spell words like "arithmetic" by reciting the little jungle *"a rat in the house might eat the ice cream."* To help remember the sequence of the colors in the spectrum, many think of *"Roy G. Biv"*—red, orange, yellow, green, blue, indigo, violet. A mnemonic helps us organize material into a logical and systematic pattern which then increases our ability to remember the material.

The use of a mnemonic device such as key words to cue the sound associated with each letter is a concept used in many fine reading programs. It is an efficient and effective teaching tool. Key words provide students with a firm base for sound/symbol associations as well as many other essential aspects of the reading process.

While presenting separate and isolated key words for each sound/symbol association is effective, it may also be laborious and tedious. Isolated key words do not have the benefit of an organized approach to their presentation. In contrast, presenting key words in an organized approach, as part of a mnemonic sentence, is both effective and efficient. The use of visual images linked to each sentence greatly enhances recall ability, and students are then able to learn the appropriate key words at an accelerated rate.

Why did I develop MFR?

After several years of experience using reading programs with isolated key words, I noticed that some children did not easily remember the key words. Their faulty memory pattern created difficulties for them in using the concept of the key word as a signal to recall the sound of a letter. These children required much drilling to develop this concept to an automatic level. I firmly believe in the value of having a key word as a *hook* to facilitate retrieval of a given sound, as does the staff at the Richards Educational Therapy Center. Out of this dilemma grew the notion of the visual mnemonic system.

We selected a visual mnemonic system because so many of our students have visual and visual-spatial strengths. Many of them are quite artistic, which creates an interesting combination with their dyslexic patterns. We realized that it was quite easy for them to visualize and remember the silly mnemonic pictures and sayings. Once this was automatic, it was easy to use these hooks to enhance sound/symbol relationships.

We hope that you will have as much success with your students as we have had with ours!

Regina G. Richards
1997

MEMORY FOUNDATIONS FOR READING

Development of efficient sound/symbol correspondences is an important aspect of the learning to read process. As a critical part of an appropriately balanced approach, it is supported in many state frameworks. While phonics should not be the sole focus of teaching or result in an overemphasis on the development of skills in isolation, phonics is critical and cannot be overlooked, or left to implicit learning. This is true for all students, most especially the dyslexic learner.

To become skillful readers, children need to learn how to decode words instantly and effortlessly. Automaticity is a major goal. Initially, they must be taught to examine the letters and letter patterns of every new word while reading. It is poor practice to teach children to skip new words or to guess their meaning, especially at the beginning stages. Research reveals that only poor and disabled readers rely on context for word identification and points to the fact that poorly developed knowledge of spellings and sound/symbol correspondences is found to be the most frequent debilitating and pervasive cause of reading difficulty (Stanovich 1980).

The most effective phonics instruction is *explicit* (Reading Program Advisory 1996, 6). This means that the key points and principles are clarified precisely for students. Anther important aspect of effective phonics instruction is that it is *systematic*: it gradually builds from basic elements to more subtle and complex patterns. The goal is to convey the logic of the system and to invite its extension to new words that children will encounter on their own.

The most effective phonics instruction is:

- Explicit
- Systematic

These needs were first substantiated by Samuel T. Orton, M.D., and Anna Gillingham, a psychologist, in their initial work on dyslexia in the early 1920's, and subsequently in Gillingham's reading program (Gillingham 1968). Teaching phonics opportunistically by pointing out sound/symbol connections only as they arise does not have the same impact on learning. While there are some students who will learn to read no matter what is done in the classroom, the dyslexic student or the student with other reading-based learning differences will not learn to read by teaching phonics opportunisti-

Orton & Gillingham: initial pioneers in teaching reading to dyslexics

● Samuel Torrey Orton, the physician who was responsible for the recognition of dyslexia as a specific learning disability in the U.S., was first to consider that the disorder might have a neural substrate (Chase 1996, 1).

● Dr. Orton stressed prognostic optimism as early as 1925 (Rawson 1995, 63).

● In the 1930s, Dr. Orton worked with Anna Gillingham, a psychologist, and Bessie Stillman, a master teacher, to develop the Orton/ Gillingham Approach (Rawson 1995, xiv).

● The Gillingham Manuals made available a systematic presentation of the structure of the English language. It described methodical procedures for teaching by the simultnaeous use of the sense of sight, hearing, and muscular awareness. But it was also adaptable in pace and detail to the individual needs and interests of the child, and to the ingenuity of the teacher who could use it as a base of operations to which other material could be added. It was an *approach*, not a *method* or a *system* (Rawson 1995, 63).

cally. This is a critical concept in understanding how to increase effective teaching of reading.

Students must first understand how the alphabetical principle works, and they need to understand the concept and use of a code system. After this understanding is entrenched, it is relatively easy for them to add new sound/symbol pairs to their working knowledge set. This is especially true for dyslexics and is the rationale for the systematic approach as initially represented by Gillingham. Initial phonics instruction is best conducted with a relatively small set of consonants and short vowels, developing sound/symbol relationships progressively. By using a limited set of letters to build as many familiar words as possible, students become more aware of the code system and learn to use phonics to read and spell logically.

The sequence of sounds presented in the MFR system is based upon the sequence of sounds as presented in the Gillingham program. There is no magical reason for this sequence. What is important is to separate presentation of letters that are similar in visual configurations (such as *b* and *d*) and sounds that are similar and difficult to discriminate (such as short *e* and short *i*). One sound in the pair should be taught and developed to a level of automaticity before the second sound is introduced. Once the second sound is introduced, substantial discrimination practice needs to be included.

Value of Sound/Symbol Associations

Many students learn to form associations between sounds and symbols through exposure, drill and practice. Dyslexic students and others who may struggle with the reading process benefit substantially by receiving direct instruction to help them form associations between visual, auditory, and kinesthetic modes. In this way, they are able to make specific links and connections between information that is auditory (what they hear), visual (what they see), and kinesthetic (what they say and write). They then can practice these connections to a level of automaticity. Gillingham referred to these multisensory links as the language triangle (see Figure 1), and use of this multisensory approach fits in quite well with a variety of reading approaches.

Key words help students recall the associations between sound and symbol. They can be explained to the students as very important helper words: they are like "keys" to help learn and remember what sound goes with each letter. While presenting separate and isolated key words for each sound/symbol association is effective, it is also laborious and tedious. Isolated key words that are not presented within a context remain isolated. In contrast, presenting key words in an organized approach is effective and efficient and allows students to use a variety of modalities for learning.

Use of key words within a mnemonic sentence provides a memory tool while incorporating a linguistic hook or connection. Use of visual images linked to each sentence enhances recall ability and pulls in visual spatial capabilities. Students then learn the appropriate key words at an accelerated rate. When the pictures are colored, additional visual input is provided. By coloring the pictures themselves, students reinforce the connections kinesthetically while learning the associated phrases.

Mnemonic strategies are critical for dyslexic learners. Mnemonics can be any technique assisting or designated to assist memory.

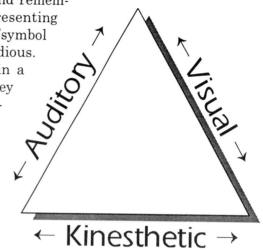

Figure 1

The basic principle of the language triangle is to build letter sounds into words, like bricks built into a wall. The technique is based upon close association of visual, auditory, and kinesthetic elements (Gillingham 1968, 40).

The MFR system of picture mnemonics provides a multidimensional organizational system divided into three sets.

- **Set one** involves the main sound for each alphabet letter
- **Set two** provides letters with multiple sounds
- **Set three** provides sounds with multiple spellings

Some less frequent sound/symbol associations (digraphs and blends) in the English language have been omitted from MFR, because it is felt that once a student reaches a certain level of proficiency, he can then easily learn the remaining sounds and generalizations. Figure 2 lists these pictures. The actual drawings are in the Appendix.

A mnemonic is a memory trick—

a strategy to provide a hook to hang on to and later retrieve a memory.

Developing Automatic Associations

Some students may need very directed assistance to develop sound/symbol correspondence. It is recommended that this assistance be provided by focusing on the concept of the language triangle. Three different associations should be used, with each activity focusing on a different sensory system. To facilitate this practice, the teacher should create letter cards,

Figure 2

List of Mnemonic Pictures

Set 1: *Main Sound: this list includes the primary sound for each letter*

1.1   tiny monkeys kiss fat pig

1.2   apple Ed is on umbrella

1.3   bunnies jump high

1.4   goat licks nine rocks

1.5   these chickens saw shadows

1.6   doll with yellow whistle vacuums zebra

1.7   qu and x: queen fox

1.8   Vowel-e: Eve types, "Huge snake broke bike"

1.9   Vowel-r: she stirs tar with her purple horn

Set 2: *Multiple Sounds: this list identifies multiple sounds for each*

2.1   Vowel y: Lynn and fly eat candy

2.2   c   city cat and country cat

2.3   g   George goat

2.4   s   saw rose

2.5   ch   chicken chef washes Christopher

2.6   th   these thumbs

2.7   a   apple watches baby fall

2.8   i   this is tiger

2.9   e   demon Ed

2.10 o   Tony on money

2.11 u   Ruby with umbrella on bugle bush

2.12 oo   hook the moon

Set 3: *Multiple Spellings: this list identifies multiple sounds for each*

3.1   /f/   fat Phillip

3.2   /k/   Christopher cat kisses duck

3.3   /j/   George jumps

3.4   /ch/ chickens hatch

3.5   /ā/   baby sprays paint on the snake

3.6   /ā/   Hey, eight great veins

3.7   /ē/   demon eats sweets

3.8   /ē/   Eve and the chief catch candy from the ceiling

3.9	/ĕ/	**Ed** has br**ead**
3.10	/ī/	fl**y** and t**i**ger on b**ike**
3.11	/ī/	p**ie** types "**igh**" words
3.12	/ĭ/	th**i**s **is** Lynn
3.13	/ō/	arr**ow** T**o**ny br**o**ke the b**oa**t with his t**oe**
3.14	/ŏ/	w**a**tches are **o**n
3.15	/ū/	h**u**ge **Eu**gene resc**u**es a f**ew** b**u**gles
3.16	/ŭ/	m**o**ney **u**mbrella
3.17	/ōō/	R**u**by thr**ew** the pr**u**ne s**ou**p at the bl**ue** m**oo**n
3.18	/oo/	h**oo**k b**u**sh
3.19	/s/	**g**iant **s**aw**s** **c**ity
3.20	/z/	**z**ebra ro**s**e
3.21	/sh/	**ch**ef's **sh**adow
3.22	/ȯ/	P**au**l f**a**lls into str**aw**s
3.23	/oi/	**oi**l b**oy**
3.24	/ou/	**ou**t c**ow**!

which may be small cards, such as 3x4 or 3x5 cards, with one letter written per card. The letters should be written in large, clear manuscript. On the reverse side, the key word for each sound made by the letter should be written, as well as a reference to the appropriate MFR picture(s). For example, the "*a*" card would have the following listing on the reverse:

apple, 1.2, 2.7

watches, 2.7, 3.14

baby, 2.7, 3.5

fall, 2.7, 3.22

A list of the cards with their labels is provided in Figure 3.

There are three main associations:

Association 1: Emphasis on visual association

Association 2: Emphasis on auditory association

Association 3: Emphasis on kinesthetic association

Each association is performed with the packet of target sounds or letters that have been introduced and taught. As more associations are added, the packet is extended.

Figure 3

A Listing of Cards Needed

Letter for Front of Card	Listing for Reverse Side	Letter for Front of Card	Listing for Reverse Side
t	tiny, 1.1	ch	chickens, 1.5, 2.5, 3.4
m	monkeys, 1.1		chef, 2.5, 3.21
k	kiss, 1.1, 3.2		Christopher, 2.5, 3.2
f	fat, 1.1, 3.1	s	saw, 1.5, 2.4, 3.19
p	pig, 1.1		rose, 2.4, 3.20
a	apple, 1.2, 2.7	sh	shadows, 1.5, 3.21
	watches, 2.7, 3.14	d	doll, 1.6
	baby, 2.7, 3.5	w	with, 1.6
	fall, 2.7, 3.22	wh	whistle, 1.6
e	Ed, 1.2, 2.9, 3.9	v	vacuums, 1.6
	demon, 2.9, 3.7	z	zebra, 1.6, 3.20
i	is, 1.2, 2.8, 3.12	qu	queen, 1.7
	tiger, 2.8, 3.10	x	fox, 1.7
o	on, 1.2, 2.10, 3.14	a-e	snake, 1.8, 3.5
	Tony, 2.10, 3.13	e-e	Eve, 1.8, 3.8
	money, 2.10, 3.16	i-e	bike, 1.8, 3.10
u	umbrella, 1.2, 2.11, 3.16	p-e	broke, 1.8, 3.13
	Ruby, 2.11, 3.17	u-e	huge, 1.8, 3.15
	bugle, 2.11, 3.15	y-e	types, 1.8, 3.11
	bush, 2.11, 3.18	ar	tar, 1.9
b	bunnies, 1.3	er	her, 1.9
j	jump, 1.3, 3.3	ir	stirs, 1.9
h	high, 1.3	or	horn, 1.9
g	goat, 1.4, 2.3	ur	purple, 1.9
	George, 2.3, 3.3	y (vowel)	Lynn, 2.1, 3.12
l	licks, 1.4		fly, 2.1, 3.10
n	nine, 1.4		candy, 2.1, 3.8
r	rocks, 1.4	c	city, 2.2, 3.19
th	these, 1.5, 2.6		cat. 2.2, 3.2
	thumbs, 2.6	oo	hooks, 2.12, 3.18
			moon, 2.12, 3.17

This listing can be used to make the letter cards needed to perform the three associations. On the front of each card, place the letter (or letters in the case of digraphs, vowel-e, and vowel-r). On the reverse side, place corresponding key words and references to MFR pictures.

These exercises should be practiced until students achieve a level of automaticity, especially since automaticity is a critical aspect for the dyslexic and dysgraphic learners (Richards 1997). Even when they reach a level of automaticity, the students need continued periodic practice to maintain the skills at an automatic level. However, once students begin to reach a minimal level of comfort and familiarity, they need to also practice using the sounds in decoding and encoding activities.

Association 1: The Visual Association

This is an important prerequisite skill for decoding words, using a code system for *reading*. There are three steps to the association: the name, the sound, and the integration with the key word. For each step, the child should go through the target pack of cards.

STEP 1 - THE NAME

♦ Child sees a letter card and says the name of the letter.

Example dialog:

Teacher: *(showing* m *card)* Tell me the name of this letter.
Student: *m*
Teacher: *(showing* t *card)* What is the name of this letter?
Student: *t*

STEP 2 - THE SOUND

♦ Child sees a letter card and says the sound of the letter.

Example dialog:

Teacher: *(showing* m *card)* Tell me the sound of this letter.
Student: /m/
Teacher: *(showing* t *card)* What is the sound of this letter?
Student: /t/

STEP THREE - THE INTEGRATION

♦ Child sees a letter card and says the letter name, key word, and sound.

Example dialog:

Teacher: *(showing* m *card)* Tell me this key word and sound.
Student: *m*, monkeys, /m/
Teacher: *(showing* j *card)*
Student: *j*, jump, /j/

When a student has progressed to a point where he has learned varied mnemonic pictures related to a given letter, then the following expanded exercise may be used to increase automaticity.

Teacher: *(showing* i *card)* What is the name, key word, and sound of this letter?
Student: *i* is /ĭ/, *i* tiger /ī/
Teacher: *(showing* o*)* This letter?
Student: *o* on /ŏ/, *o* Tony /ō/, *o* monkey /ŭ/

Association 2: The Auditory Association

This is an important prerequisite skill to encoding, or *spelling*. The child hears the sound and gives the name of the letter, or he hears the name and then provides the sound. In this association, he does not look at the cards.

Example one: Student hears letter name and says its sound (no cards are used)

Teacher:	What's the sound of *p*?
Student:	/p/
Teacher:	What's the sound of *k*?
Student:	/k/

Or, as an alternative when the student is accustomed to the drill technique:

Teacher:	*m*
Student:	/m/
Teacher:	*a*
Student:	/ă/

Example two: Emphasis on the student giving the letter name.

Teacher:	What letter has the /p/ sound?
Student:	*p*
Teacher:	What letter has the /t/ sound?
Student:	*t*

Or,

Teacher:	/m/
Student:	*m*
Teacher:	/h/
Student:	*h*

Example three: Key words may also be used to facilitate recall of the association. For example,

Teacher:	*m*
Student:	*m*, monkey, /m/
Teacher:	*a*
Student:	*a*, apple, /ă/

Examples of expanded exercises using multiple sounds with association 2 (MFR, Set 2)

Teacher:	What are the sounds of *c*?
Student:	/s/ and /k/ or /s/ city and /k/ cat
Teacher:	What are the sounds of *ch*?
Student:	/ch/, /sh/, and /k/ for /ch/ chicken, /sh/ chef, and /k/ Christopher

Examples of expanded exercises using multiple spellings with association 2 (MFR, set 3)

Teacher:	What letters have the /f/ sound?
Student:	*f* as in fat and *ph* as in Phillip
Teacher:	The /k/ sound?
Student:	*k* as in kisses, *c* as in cat, *ch* as in Christopher, and *ck* as in duck

Association 3: The Kinesthetic Association

During this procedure, the student traces, copies, or *writes* the letter after hearing either the letter name or the letter sound. The student is to say the letter name as she traces or writes the letter to help solidify the link. For example,

Teacher:	Write *m*.
Student:	*(writes the letter* m, *saying)* /m/

or,

Teacher:	Write the letter that has the /m/ sound.
Student:	*(writes the letter* m, *saying)* /m/

The exercises used here are the same as for Association 1, the visual association. The difference is that the student simultaneously writes and says her response. The student can vary the writing practice by:

- Tracing letters written large on a chalkboard (using a vertical plane)

- Writing the letters in the air relying more on his own bodily-kinesthetic modalities

- Writing the letter independently on paper

A variety of activities should be used at different points within the learning sequence. Air writing is of critical importance for dyslexic and dysgraphic students and serves several purposes. Air writing (or any writing) while saying the name has multisensory impact: it connects a motor movement with vision (seeing the letter card) and with auditory (hearing yourself say the name). It also serves to strengthen the motor memory for the form of the letter, providing large muscle input. Students can be encouraged to imagine the letter as they air write it, thus strengthening their imaging skill, which will lead to greater automaticity. In addition, it is an efficient group teaching technique since it allows the teacher to monitor several students at once. When the students respond on paper, the teacher is only able to monitor the end product, not the process, for most of the students. When introducing air writing to the students, tell them,

- This time when you say the letter name, I want you to write the letter *t* in the air.

- Write it big.

- Use two fingers as your "pointer" and keep your wrist and elbow fairly straight.

- I want you to be able to really feel the movements you make while you are writing the *t* in the air.

- I will write it with you.

- (Teacher needs to stand facing the class and make her *t* backwards so that the students may follow the movements.)

- Now, class, say the key word and sound for this letter as we write it in the air.

- Class: air writes *t*, saying, "*t*, tiny, /t/."

- Teacher: "Can you imagine the letter in the air where you wrote it? See it there."

If students struggle to visualize the letter, have them try variations such as:

- Imagine a shadow that stays where you wrote the *t*.

- Imagine writing your letter using bright red Silly String®.

- Imagine your letter in the air made of thick spaghetti. Trace its form.

Variations on the Primary Associations Using Other Modalities and Techniques

These activities often incorporate more than one learning modality. For example, feeling the sounds and organizing them into patterns pulls in bodily-kinesthetic activities as well as emphasizing the logical patterns. This aspect of integration is an important component of the multiple intelligences paradigm.

Bodily-kinesthetic modalities

- Students dance or sway and clap to music while the teacher calls out a letter name. Students say the key word and letter sound until the teacher calls the next letter.

- Teacher calls out a letter name and the students place a partner into a shape to represent that letter. Once the partner student is in the shape, that student says the letter sound. Key words can be added.

- Teacher calls out a letter name and all the students form their bodies into that letter and then say its sound.

- Students practice any of the three associations while jumping on a trampa, a small mini-trampoline (also called rebounder or exerciser).
- Students create jump rope rhythms, utilizing the name of the letter, sounds, and key words

Musical-rhythmic intelligences

- Students create a rap incorporating the name, sound, and key word
- Students create a song incorporating the key words or mnemonic phrase, such as the following:

   "Apple Ed's a funny fella, likes to sit on his umbrella"

Logical-mathematical patterns

- Student organizes sounds into linguistic pairs by focusing on feeling the sounds as they are made in the mouth. Structured suggestions on emphasizing this type of modality are readily found in programs such as Lindamood's *Auditory Discrimination in Depth*. For example, a pair made by putting the lips together and popping the sound out (lip poppers) is *b* and *p*. Long *e* and short *i* are both called smile sounds because of the position of the mouth (Lindamood 1975)

Visual Spatial activities

- Students make letters out of clay or other art supplies
- Students make a collage of pictures starting with a given sound
- Students work letter puzzles

Manipulative Patterns for Chaining

For students who struggle substantially, it is best to initially teach the first five consonants (*t,m,k,f,p*) and one short vowel (as in *a*, apple, /a/). At that point, the teacher can use letter cards or magnetic letters to create a variety of letter combinations that the students can decode (read) or encode (spell). For encoding, the teacher can say a sound pattern or a syllable, and the students manipulate the letters to spell the word. For the decoding (reading) activity, the teacher can create the combination and let the students read it, or one student can make a combination for the other students.

As more sounds are introduced, it is valuable to provide some activities related to chaining of sounds. This can be done in a purely auditory mode to have a greater impact on phonological awareness, or it can be performed using visual clues. Variety is valuable. Chaining activities are useful for all children, as it helps develop an ability to manipulate sounds, an important aspect of phonological awareness.

Figure 4

Chaining Patterns

Activity 1, using letters

Teacher:	(creates the word "mat" with magnetic letters and guides the students to sound out the word) Right, this is mat. What happens if we take away the *m* and put in *h*? What sound does *h* have?
Students:	/h/
Teacher:	What is the new word?
Students:	hat
Teacher:	What happens if we take out the /t/ and put in a /p/ sound?
Students:	hat (take out *t*) - ha (add *p*) p
Teacher:	What is the new word?
Students:	hap

Activity 2, using visual cues without letters (such as blocks or squares)

Teacher:	Listen to this pattern: cap. Show me how many sounds you hear.
Students:	/k/ /a/ /p/—I hear three sounds (places three different colored blocks on table)
Teacher:	Good. Now, what changes if I change cap to tap?
Students:	(pointing to first sound) This one. (Removes first block and substitutes a different color)
Teacher:	Say the new word.
Students:	tap

Activity 3, auditory mode

Teacher:	Repeat this word: sit
Students:	sit
Teacher:	Change /s/ to /p/. What do you have?
Students:	pit
Teacher:	Change /i/ to /a/. What do you have?
Students:	pat

As more vowels are incorporated, the middle sound can also be changed. It is important to explain to students that many of these may not be real words, but they are logical combinations of sounds and letters that could occur in real words, especially in much longer words. It is important to use nonsense words to bypass the memory system and encourage the students to focus more completely on analysis.

As students progress and are familiar with more letters, it is fun to write a very long phonetically logical word containing only those letters on the chalkboard. Define a syllable as a unit having a vowel and help them divide the long word into syllables and then sound it out. Technically, a syllable is a unit of spoken language consisting of an uninterrupted utterance and forming either a whole word (as cat) or a commonly recognized division of a word. Example words include the following:

- abominable
- anatomically
- interdependent
- predestination
- reincarnation
- representation
- transmigrational
- uneducated

Discussion of the words' meanings and affixes (prefixes and suffixes) will help enhance the students' learning.

Using the Mnemonics

Following are suggestions for using MFR mnemonics as the means for introducing key words. A letter is introduced, as in the following dialogue.

Teacher: Today we are going to learn about the letter *m*. It has the sound /m/. Tell me some words that start with the /m/ sound.

Students: *(List a variety of words starting with /m/ sound while teacher writes suggestions on the board.)*

Teacher: *(teacher guides students until one of them names monkey.)* Yes, all of these words are good, and one of the words is *monkey*. Let's look at this picture. This picture says 'tiny monkeys kiss fat pig.' Do you see the monkeys? What's the sound at the beginning of monkeys?

Students: /m/

Teacher: We are going to use the word monkeys to help us remember that the letter m has the /m/ sound. Everybody repeat: *m*, monkeys, /m/.

Students: *m*, monkey, /m/

Teacher: Good. Now every time we think of the letter *m*, we can also remember monkeys and remember *m* has the /m/ sound.

Additional Teaching Strategy: Discovery

Many students benefit from the use of a discovery technique since this pulls in higher level thinking skills. To use discovery with MFR, show an MFR picture, covering up the sentence. Ask, "What do you think the sentence that goes with this picture is?" Example (using MFR 1.3 "bunnies jump high"):

Teacher: What do you see here?

Student: Bunnies.

Teacher: What are they doing?

Student: Flying.

Teacher: Are the bunnies flying in this picture? They don't have wings. What else could they be doing? *(Example of error questioning)*

Student: I guess they are jumping.

Teacher: Good. Are these bunnies jumping low?

Student: No.

Teacher: How are they jumping?

Student: High.

Teacher: So what do you think this picture could be?

Student: Bunnies jump high.

It is important that questions be set up within a narrow framework to elicit the desired response.

Potential Problems in Teaching MFR

1.   Sequence of Motor Movements

Some young students and those with dyslexia or dysgraphia may have difficulties remembering how to form specific letters. Many times the difficulty is due to poor recall of the sequence of motor movements. In this case, a valuable technique is to teach the students to "auditorize" the steps necessary for the formation of each letter (it works for numerals, too!). For example, *t* is "tall stick down, lift up, and across." *d* is "round like an *a,* big tall stick." *b* is "tall stick down, circle away from my body" (for right handers) or "tall stick down, circle in front of my body" (for left handers). These verbal clues may be recited by the class and teacher during air writing or chalkboard work. Verbal cues are also a great aid towards eliminating reversal problems.

2.   Identifying Initial Sounds

For most students, the concept of key words may be initiated easily. However, some students have difficulty utilizing this concept because they have not yet learned to separate out sounds within a word, usually due to phonological awareness gaps. These students need to start with the identification of initial sounds. A sequence for teaching would be:

1. Teach the concepts of 'beginning" and "first." Use concrete materials and gross motor movements.
2. Use exaggerated speech while asking the students to identify the beginning sound. E.g., /t . . . i . . . ne/
3. Use regular speech and ask students to identify the beginning sound.

3.   Blending

Introduce blending skills after the introduction of pictures 1.1 and 1.2. Some students may be able to "read the sounds" but be unable to blend them together. A visual cue may be extremely valuable in teaching the concept of "bringing the sounds together." For example, with the word **am** a slide is drawn:

The teacher then takes her hand and "slides" the *a* down to the *m,* saying /a---m/, /am/, using voicing to indicate that the /a/ slides down and joins with the /m/.

4.   Concept of "Sounds" as Used in Association Drills

Some children quickly rote learn the sequence such as "*t*, /t/, tiny" but are still unable to respond to questions such as, "What is the sound of *t*?" These children require much practice with the Association Drills, using only one step at a time. In addition, they benefit from activities designed to teach that "things make sounds." Progress from concrete objects and animals, e.g., dog, bell, keys, etc., to the idea that the letter *t* is a "thing" and it, too, makes a sound. The sound is /t/.

5.   Schwa /ə/ After Consonants

Many children have a tendency towards adding the schwa /ə/ sound after a consonant when saying isolated sounds, e.g., /buh/ for /b/ and /tuh/ for /t/. It is critical to help them, through appropriate modeling and gentle corrections, to make isolated sounds without adding the schwa. Otherwise, when blending a word such as **mat,** they will end up with /muh . . . a . . . t/. [Note: a schwa sound is an unaccented vowel sound, similar to short /u/.]

Bibliography

Chase, Christopher H., Rosen, Glenn D., & Sherman, Gordon F., 1996. *Developmental Dyslexia: Neural, Cognitive & Genetic Mechanisms*. Baltimore, MD: York Press.

Fletcher, J.M., Francis, D.J., Rourke, B.P., Shaywitz, S.E., & Shaywitz, B.A., 1993. Classification of learning disabilities: Relationships with other childhood disorders. In G.R. Lyon, D.B. Gray, J.F. Kavanagh, & N.A. Krasnegor (Eds.). *Better understanding learning disabilities: New views form research and their implications for education and public policies*. Baltimore: Paul H. Brookes Publishing Co.

Gillingham, Anna, and Stillman, Bessie, 1968. *Remedial Training for Children with Specific Disability in Reading, Spelling, and Penmanship*. MA: Educator's Publishing Service.

Lindamood, C.H., and Lindamood, P.C., 1975. *Auditory Discrimination in Depth*. Austin, TX: Pro-Ed.

Rawson, Margaret B., 1995. *Dyslexia Over the Lifespan: A 55-year longitudinal study*. MA: Educator's Publishing Service.

Reading Program Advisory, 1996. *Teaching Reading: A Balanced, Comprehensive Approach to Teaching Reading in Pre-Kindergarten Through Grade Three*. Sacramento, CA: CA Dept. of Education Publishing.

Richards, Regina, 1993. *LEARN: Playful Techniques to Accelerate Learning*. Tucson, AZ: Zephyr Press.

Richards, Regina, 1997. *Dysgraphia: The Writing Dilemma*. CA: RET Center Press.

Stanovich, Keith E., 1994. Romance & Reality. *The Reading Teacher*, Vol. 47, #4, 280-291.

Stanovich, K.E., 1980. Toward an interactive-compensatory model of individual differences in the development of reading fluency. *Reading Research Quarterly* 16, 32-71.

Yopp, H., 1992. *Developing Phonemic Awareness in Young Children. The Reading Teacher*. Vol. 45, 696-703.

tiny monkeys
kiss fat pig

Memory Foundations for Learning © RET Center Press, Riverside CA

apple Ed is
on umbrella

bunnies jump high

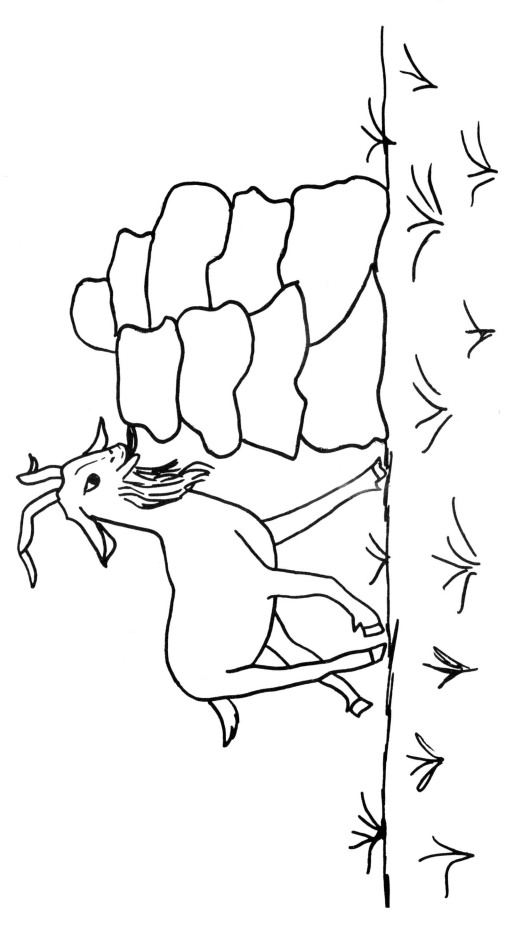

goat licks nine rocks

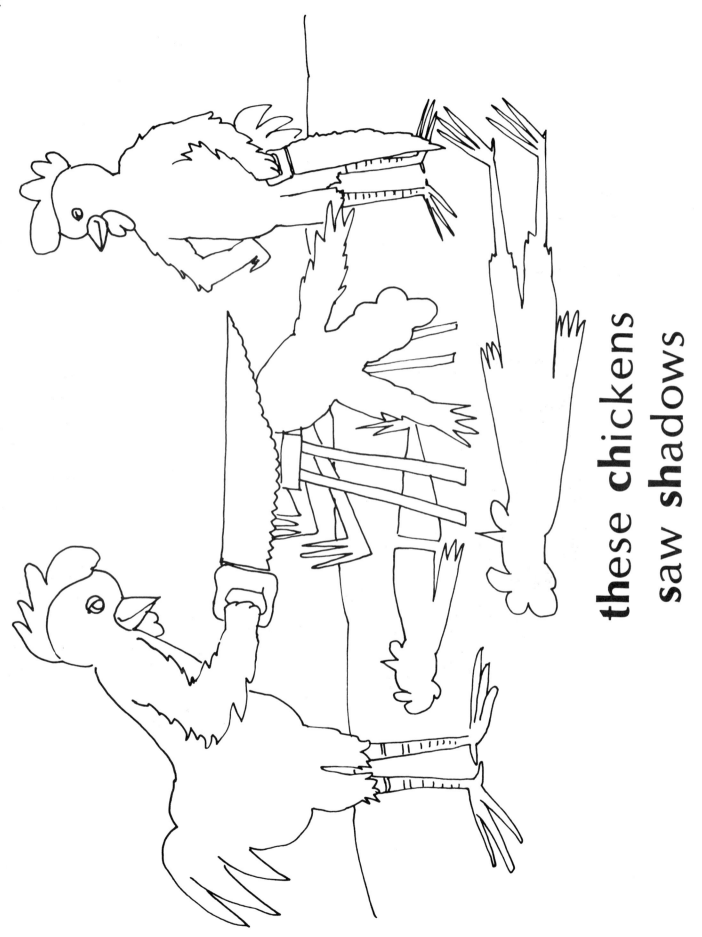

these chickens
saw shadows

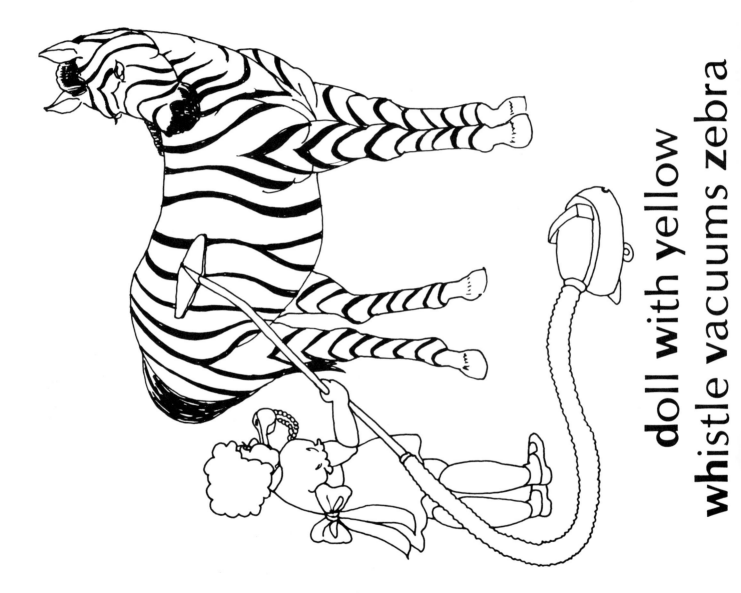

doll with yellow

whistle vacuums zebra

queen fox

Memory Foundations for Learning © RET Center Press, Riverside

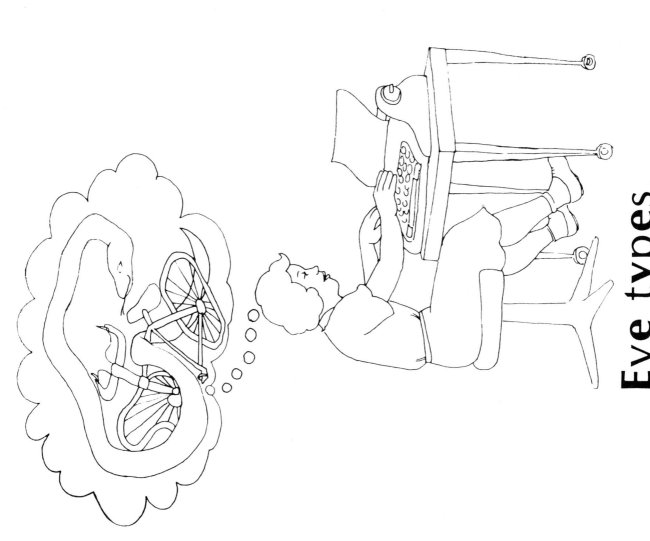

Eve types,
"Huge snake broke bike"

she stirs tar
with her purple horn

Lynn and fly
eat candy

city cat
and country cat

Memory Foundations for Learning © RET Center Press, Riverside CA

George goat

Memory Foundations for Learning © RET Center Press, Riverside CA

saw rose

Memory Foundations for Learning © RET Center Press, Riverside

chicken chef washes Christopher

Memory Foundations for Learning © RET Center Press, Riverside CA

these thumbs

apple watches
baby fall

this is tiger

Memory Foundations for Learning © RET Center Press, Riverside

demon Ed

Tony on money

Memory Foundations for Learning © RET Center Press, Riverside C

Ruby with umbrella on bugle bush

hook the moon

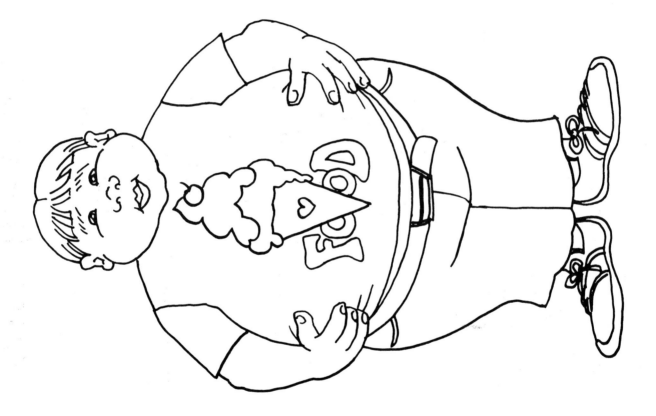

fat Phillip

Memory Foundations for Learning © RET Center Press, Riverside CA

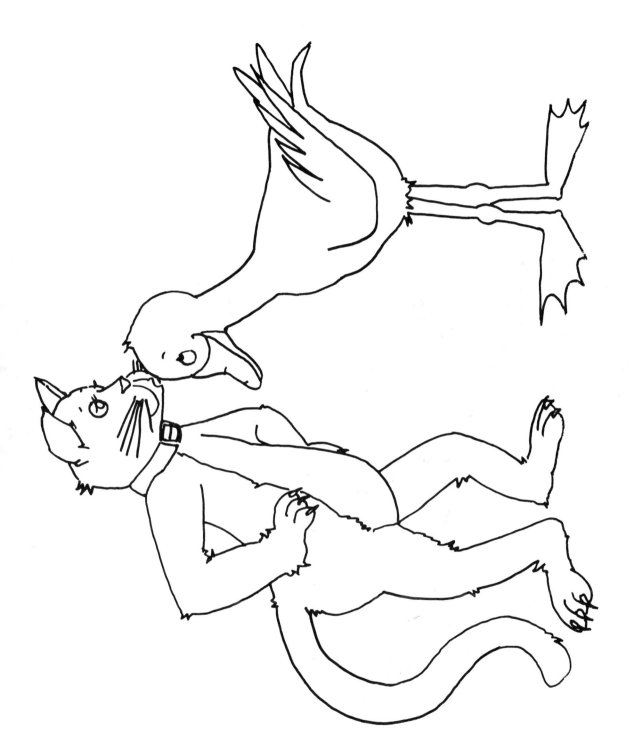

Christopher cat kisses duck

Memory Foundations for Learning © RET Center Press, Riverside CA

George jumps

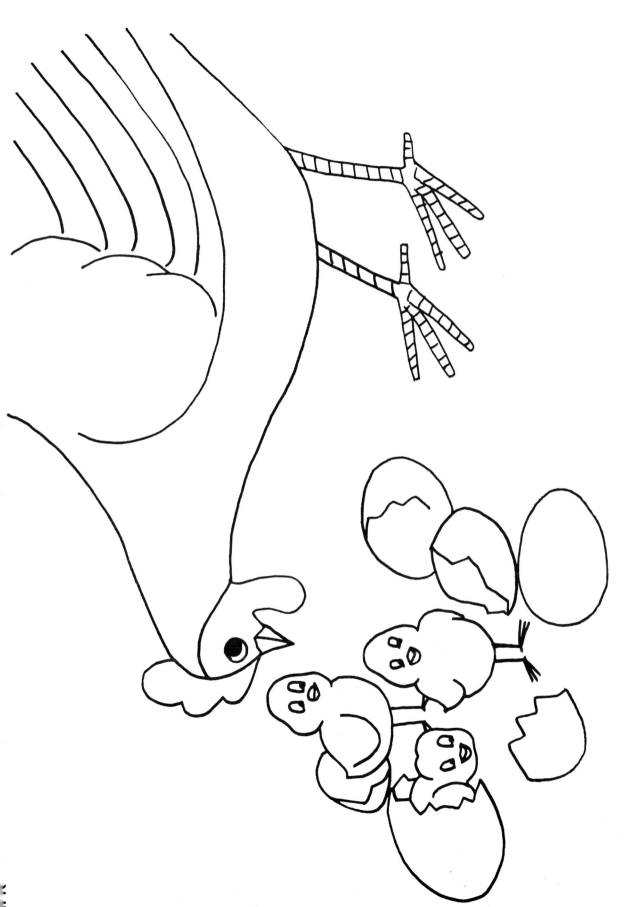

chickens hatch

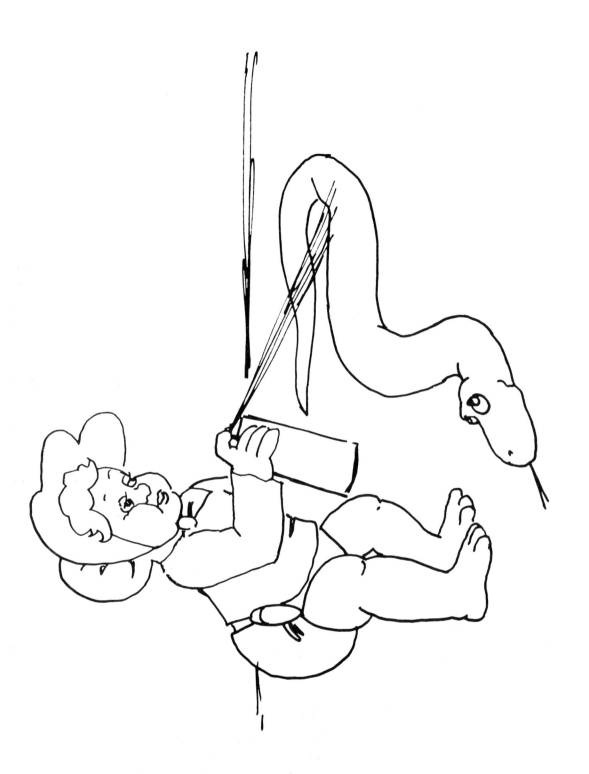

baby sprays
paint on the snake

Memory Foundations for Learning © RET Center Press, Riverside CA

hey, eight great veins

Memory Foundations for Learning © RET Center Press, Riverside C

demon eats sweets

Memory Foundations for Learning © RET Center Press, Riverside CA

Eve and the chief
catch candy from the ceiling

Memory Foundations for Learning © RET Center Press, Riverside

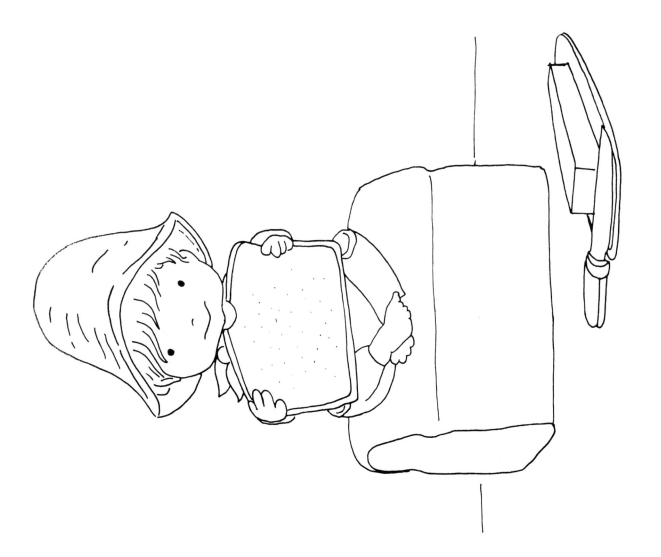

Ed has bread

Memory Foundations for Learning © RET Center Press, Riverside CA

fly and tiger on bike

Memory Foundations for Learning © RET Center Press, Riverside

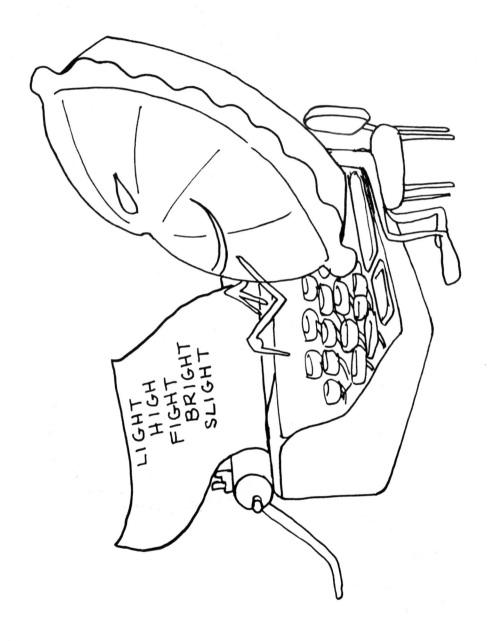

LIGHT
HIGH
FIGHT
BRIGHT
SLIGHT

pie types "igh" words

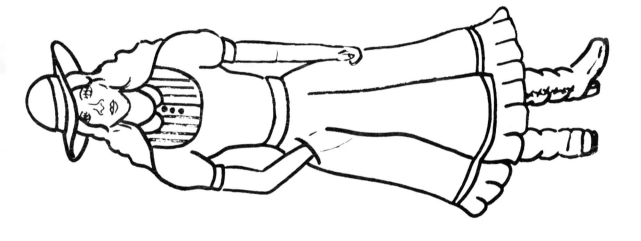

this is Lynn

Memory Foundations for Learning © RET Center Press, Riverside C

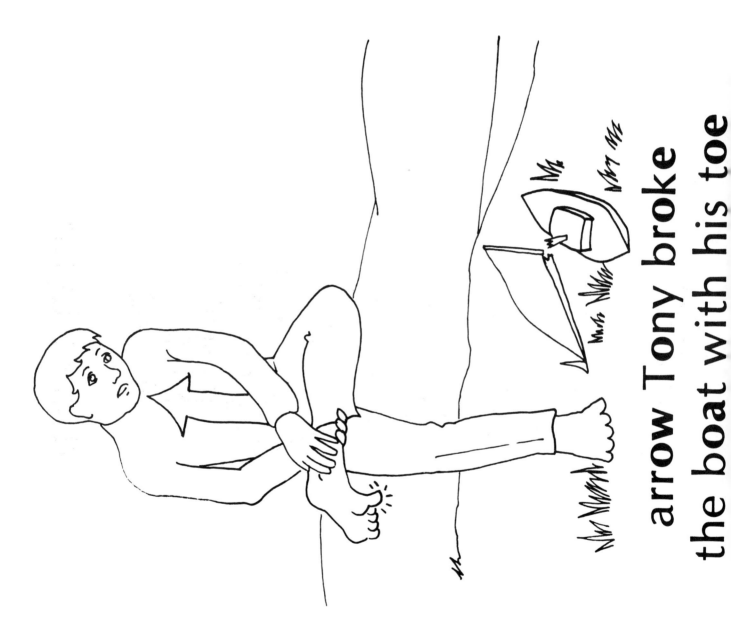

arrow Tony broke
the boat with his toe

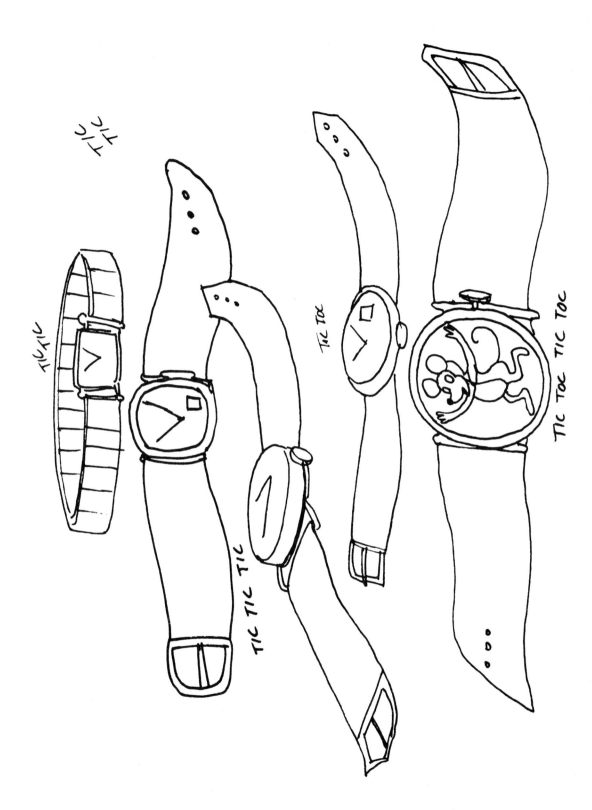

watches are on

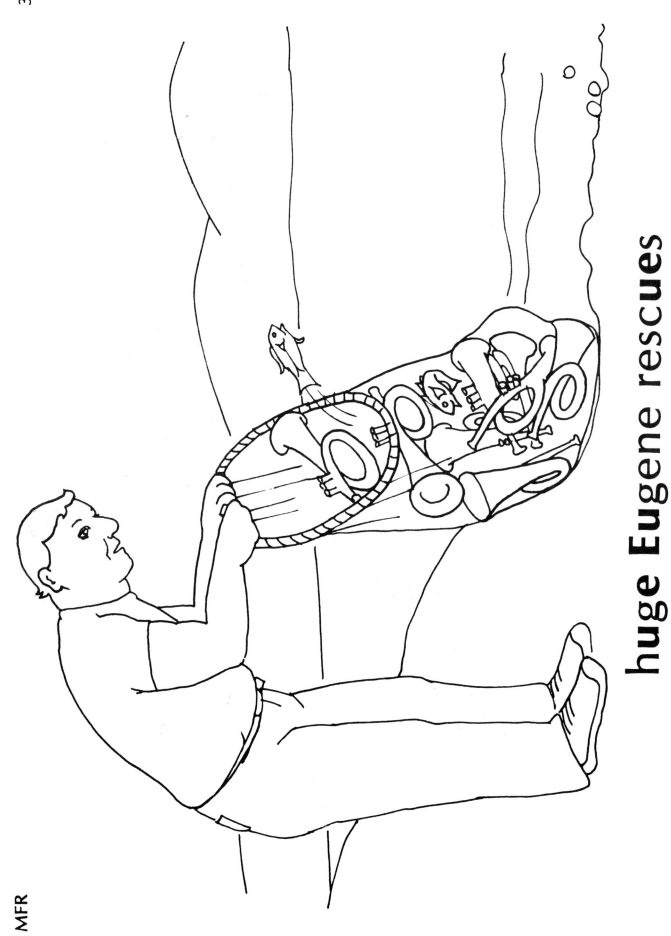

huge Eugene rescues
a few bugles

Memory Foundations for Learning © RET Center Press, Riverside CA

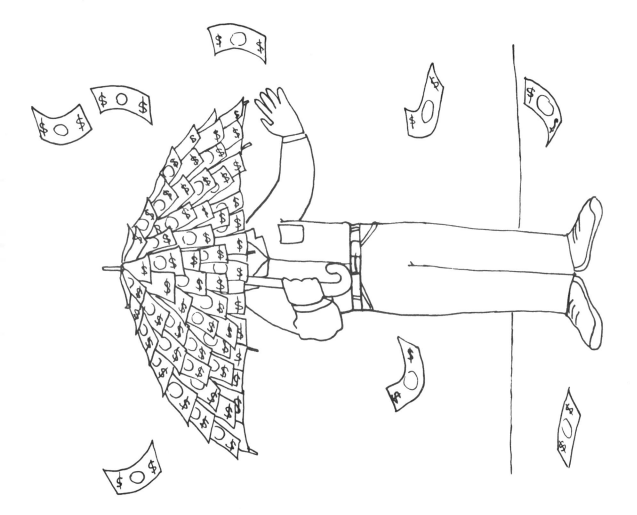

money umbrella

Memory Foundations for Learning © RET Center Press, Riverside

Ruby threw the prune soup at the blue moon

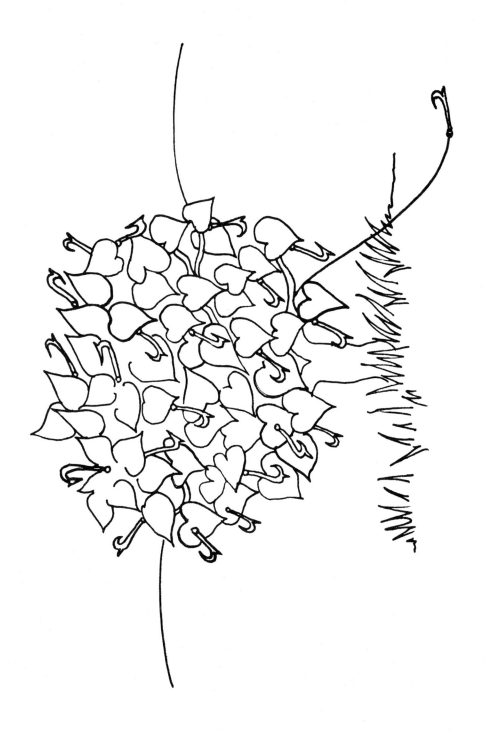

hook bush

Memory Foundations for Learning © RET Center Press, Riverside

giant saws city

zebra rose

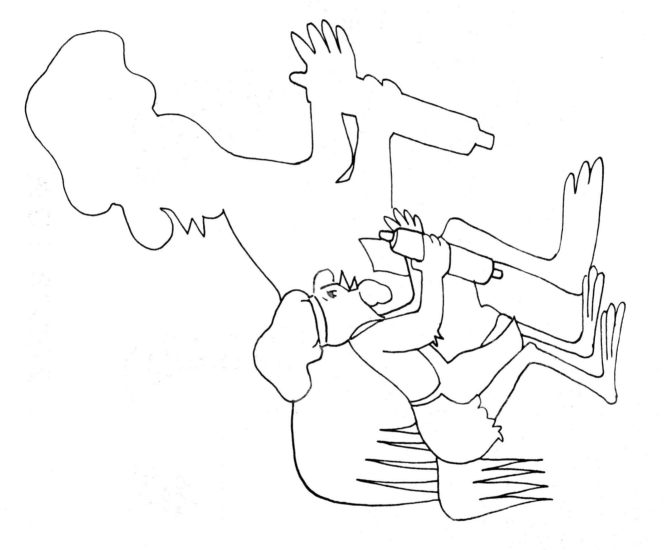

chef's shadow

Paul falls into straws

Memory Foundations for Learning © RET Center Press, Riverside C

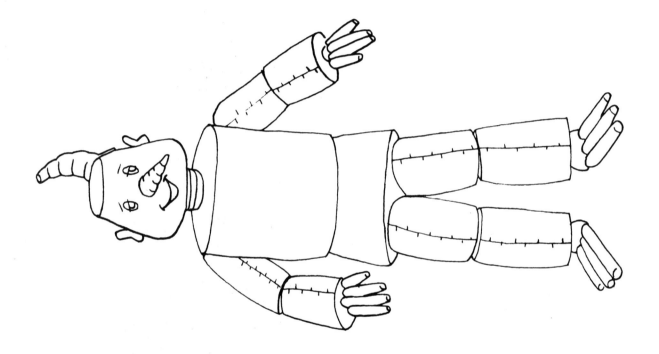

oil boy

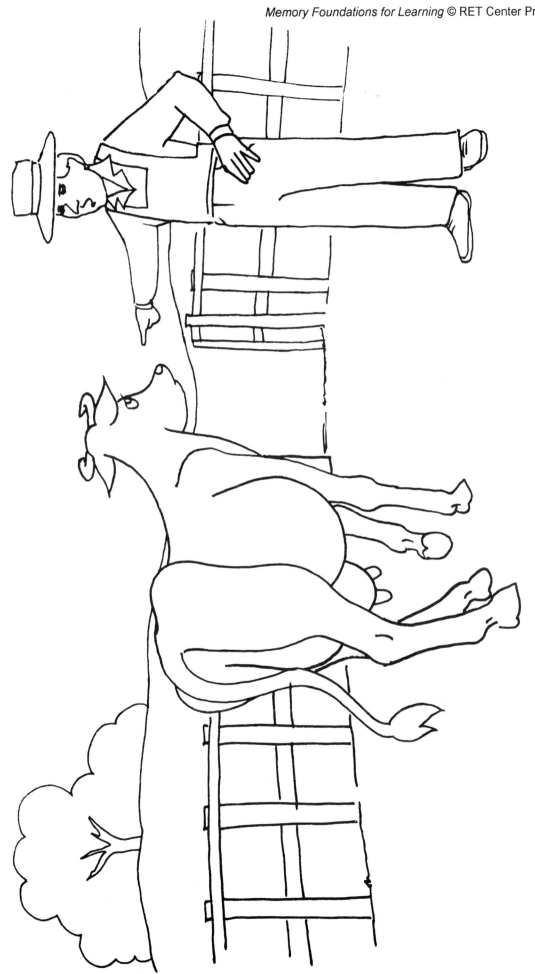

out cow!